EXPLORING COUNTRIES

Tanzania

by Emily Rose Oachs

BLASTOFF! READERS 5

BELLWETHER MEDIA • MINNEAPOLIS, MN

Note to Librarians, Teachers, and Parents:

Blastoff! Readers are carefully developed by literacy experts and combine standards-based content with developmentally appropriate text.

Level 1 provides the most support through repetition of high-frequency words, light text, predictable sentence patterns, and strong visual support.

Level 2 offers early readers a bit more challenge through varied simple sentences, increased text load, and less repetition of high-frequency words.

Level 3 advances early-fluent readers toward fluency through increased text and concept load, less reliance on visuals, longer sentences, and more literary language.

Level 4 builds reading stamina by providing more text per page, increased use of punctuation, greater variation in sentence patterns, and increasingly challenging vocabulary.

Level 5 encourages children to move from "learning to read" to "reading to learn" by providing even more text, varied writing styles, and less familiar topics.

Whichever book is right for your reader, Blastoff! Readers are the perfect books to build confidence and encourage a love of reading that will last a lifetime!

This edition first published in 2017 by Bellwether Media, Inc.

No part of this publication may be reproduced in whole or in part without written permission of the publisher. For information regarding permission, write to Bellwether Media, Inc., Attention: Permissions Department, 5357 Penn Avenue South, Minneapolis, MN 55419.

Library of Congress Cataloging-in-Publication Data

Names: Oachs, Emily Rose, author.
Title: Tanzania / by Emily Rose Oachs.
Other titles: Blastoff! Readers. 5, Exploring Countries.
Description: Minneapolis, MN : Bellwether Media, Inc., 2017. | Series:
    Blastoff! Readers: Exploring Countries | Includes bibliographical
    references and index. | Audience: Ages 7-12.
Identifiers: LCCN 2015050798 | ISBN 9781626174054 (hardcover : alk. paper)
Subjects: LCSH: Tanzania–Juvenile literature.
Classification: LCC DT438 .O22 2017 | DDC 967.8–dc23
LC record available at http://lccn.loc.gov/2015050798

Printed in the United States of America, North Mankato, MN.

Contents

On Africa's eastern coast, Tanzania stretches across 365,755 square miles (947,300 square kilometers). Its capital, Dodoma, stands in the center. The Indian Ocean crashes on the country's eastern shore. Off the coast, Tanzania's islands of Zanzibar, Pemba, and Mafia rise from the ocean.

Kenya and Uganda border northern Tanzania. Rwanda and Burundi are Tanzania's northwestern neighbors. To the west, Lake Tanganyika stands between Tanzania and the Democratic Republic of the Congo. Southwestern Tanzania touches Zambia. Lake Nyasa forms part of Tanzania's southwestern border with Malawi. Mozambique sits directly south.

Uganda

Rwanda

Burundi

Lake Tanganyika

Democratic Republic of the Congo

Zambia

4

Lake Victoria

Did you know?
The enormous Lake Victoria forms much of Tanzania's northern border with Uganda. Its area makes it the second-largest freshwater lake in the world!

Kenya

Tanzania

★
Dodoma

N
W ✦ E
S

Indian Ocean →

Malawi →

Lake Nyasa ↙

Mozambique

5

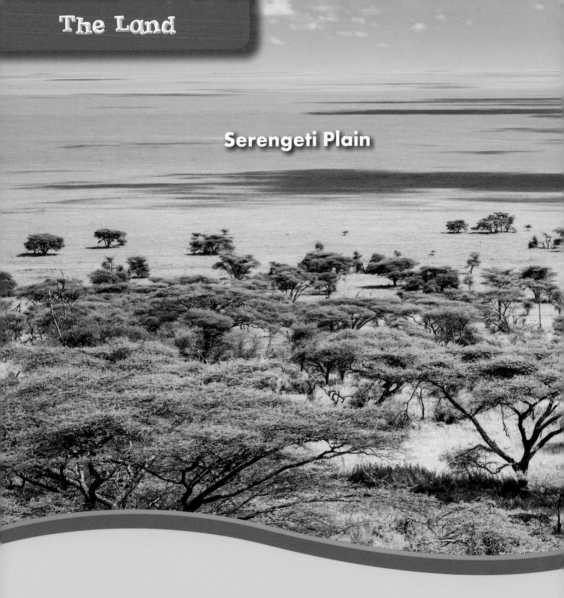

Serengeti Plain

Along the coast, low **plains** spread across the land.
This is Tanzania's warmest and rainiest region. From
the plains, the land rises into a broad **plateau** through
central Tanzania. The plateau stretches across much of
the country. Savannahs cover this hot, dry region. The
most famous, the Serengeti Plain, sits in the north between
Lake Victoria and Tanzania's eastern mountains.

The East African **Rift Valley** cuts through western and central Tanzania. This system created many of the country's northern and southern mountains. It also carved deep valleys into the earth. Many of these have filled with water to form lakes, such as Lake Tanganyika and Lake Nyasa.

East African Rift Valley

Near the border with Kenya, Mount Kilimanjaro towers over Tanzania's plains. This mountain is Africa's highest, at 19,341 feet (5,895 meters) tall. It is called the "roof of Africa." A string of three **volcanoes** forms Kilimanjaro. Two are no longer active. Kibo, the tallest, lies **dormant**. It last erupted thousands of years ago. However, it sometimes still releases steam and gas.

Snow and ice cover Kilimanjaro's highest peak year-round. But lower slopes are much warmer. The mountain and its surrounding lands are part of Kilimanjaro National Park. Forests on Kilimanjaro's southern slopes shelter elephants, elands, colobus monkeys, and duikers.

fun fact

More than 35,000 people attempt to climb to Kilimanjaro's peak each year. Only about half reach the top!

Did you know?
The Uhuru Torch was first lit on top of Mount Kilimanjaro in 1961. This important symbol of Tanzania stands for light and freedom.

flamingos

cheetah

hippopotamus

Rich, varied wildlife fills Tanzania's vast borders. Green sea turtles lay their eggs on the country's coastal beaches. On riverbanks, hippopotamuses and crocodiles soak up the hot sun. Black rhinoceroses cool off in mud puddles. Pink flamingos wade through shallow lake waters, while ostriches sprint across the Serengeti Plain.

wildebeest migration

In the grasslands, lions and cheetahs hunt antelope. Giraffes use their long tongues to pluck leaves from acacia trees. Each year, a massive animal **migration** takes place in northern Tanzania. Herds of thousands of wildebeests, zebras, and gazelles flood the Serengeti Plain. They move with the seasons to find fresh food and water.

Maasai tribe

Did you know?
To greet their elders, Tanzanian children say, "Shikamoo." In English, this means, "I hold your feet!" Saying this shows respect to the elders.

More than 51 million people call Tanzania home. Most are **native** to the area. They make up more than 120 different tribes across the country. Each tribe has its own language and **traditions**. The largest is the Sukuma. Non-native Tanzanians include small numbers of Asians and Europeans.

Tanzanians most often speak the official language of Swahili. English is also an official language. On the island of Zanzibar, Arabic is commonly heard. Most people also speak the language of their tribe. Tanzanians may practice Islam, Christianity, or a traditional African religion. About equal numbers of the population follow each religion.

Speak Swahili!

English	Swahili	How to say it
hello	hujambo	hoo-JOM-boh
goodbye	kwaheri	kwa-HAR-ee
yes	ndiyo	en-DEE-yo
no	hapana	ha-PAH-nah
please	tafadhali	ta-fah-DALL-ee
thank you	asante	ah-SAWN-tee
friend	rafiki	rah-FEE-kee

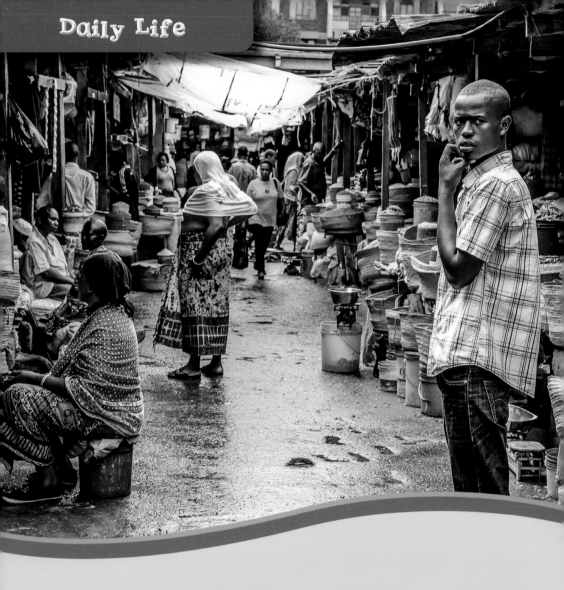

Most Tanzanians live in the countryside and work on farms. Their homes have mud or stone walls and thatched roofs. Near each home is a small field for farming called a *shamba*. In the city, Tanzanians live in small concrete or clay homes. The houses are built close together. City dwellers buy their meat, fruits, and vegetables from large marketplaces. Few Tanzanians have electricity. It is most commonly available in cities.

Most of Tanzania's roads are unpaved. Bicycles are popular in cities and the countryside. **Rural** Tanzanians also walk or ride donkeys to get from place to place. In the city, people catch rides in small, three-wheeled taxis called *bajajis*.

Where People Live in Tanzania

cities
31.6%

countryside
68.4%

Did you know?
In the countryside, Tanzanian women sometimes must fetch water from far away. They collect the water in jugs. Then they balance these jugs on their heads as they walk home!

15

Tanzanian students enter primary school around age 7. There, students learn to read and write in Swahili. They also take math, science, social studies, and the English language. After seven years, students enter secondary school. Students must go for four years, but some choose to attend for six. After graduating secondary school, most students find jobs. Some enroll in a university.

For many years, students had to pay for secondary school. Few could afford to pay the yearly fees, and they did not continue their education. However, in 2016, the government made secondary school free for all students. It is working to improve education for Tanzanian children!

Where People Work
in Tanzania

farming 82%

services 16%

manufacturing 2%

fun fact

More than a million tourists flood into Tanzania each year. They come to see the country's wildlife, enjoy its scenery, and relax on its beaches.

Farming is very important to Tanzania. About four out of every five Tanzanians are famers. Large farms plant crops to **export**, including cashews, coffee beans, and tea. On shambas, families grow crops such as corn, rice, and bananas. They also raise chickens and goats. Families rely on these crops and animals to feed themselves. In northeastern Tanzania, the Maasai people rear cattle for their food.

Many Tanzanians earn a living doing **service jobs**. They own small businesses or work in banks, schools, and shops. Others serve Tanzania's many **tourists** at hotels, restaurants, and attractions. Miners dig for gold, tin, and gemstones. In factories, workers make fabric, food products, and cement.

19

Soccer is Tanzania's most popular sport. Children and adults enjoy watching and playing the game. Basketball and boxing also have many fans. People pass the time playing cards, checkers, and the board game mancala, or *bao*. Young Tanzanians love listening to hip-hop music, called *bongo flava*. It first started in Tanzania in the 1990s.

Did you know?
Tanzania's long-distance runners are famous for their speed. The country loves to cheer them on.

Storytelling is very important to Tanzanians. Storytellers
share folktales that have been passed down through
tribes. These stories entertain the listeners. They also teach
listeners important life lessons. For the Sukuma, dancing
is another long-held tradition. Each year, they compete
in huge dance competitions. They perform their unique
dances in creative costumes.

mishkaki

Did you know?

Tanzanians always wash their hands before eating. They often pass a bowl and a towel around the table so each guest can wash up.

Ugali is among Tanzania's most common foods. It is a dough made from corn or **cassava** flour. At meals, a bowl of *ugali* usually sits at the center of the table. People reach in to grab a small piece of dough with their fingers. Then they dip it into a sauce or a stew made from vegetables or meat.

Near the coast, Tanzanians frequently serve rice with fish cooked in coconut oil. **Plantains** are popular in the northwest. In cities, street carts sell freshly squeezed cane juice, sweet potatoes, and *mishkaki*, or skewers of grilled goat or beef.

ugali

plantains

fun fact

People use their fingers to eat many Tanzanian dishes. But they only use their right hands to eat!

Tanzanian people celebrate several important national holidays. Union Day falls on April 26. On this day in 1964, Tanganyika and Zanzibar joined to create Tanzania. Independence Day takes place on December 9. It recognizes Tanganyika's independence from the British. The country celebrates these two holidays with speeches from the president, parades, and performances of traditional dance.

On December 25, Christian Tanzanians observe Christmas. They attend church services and cook special meals. Sometimes they decorate Christmas trees. Muslim Tanzanians spend the month of Ramadan **fasting** and praying. At the end, they celebrate *Eid al-Fitr* with gifts, feasts, and brightly colored clothing. This holiday lasts several days.

Union Day

25

Olduvai Gorge

On the Serengeti Plain, Olduvai Gorge holds **prehistoric** treasures. In the 1930s, **archaeologists** dug up stone tools there. Some dated back to nearly 2 million years earlier. In the 1950s and 1960s, archaeologists also uncovered bones from early human **ancestors**. The scientists guessed they were more than 1.75 million years old!

Scientists believe the first modern humans lived in Africa 200,000 years ago. The discoveries at Olduvai Gorge have helped scientists to learn how humans **evolved** from our ancestors. Today, these dig sites are open to the public. They allow visitors to see how important Tanzania is in the history of humankind.

Did you know?

At Olduvai Gorge, archaeologists found bones from prehistoric ape species. The animal lived at least 18 million years ago!

Fast Facts About Tanzania

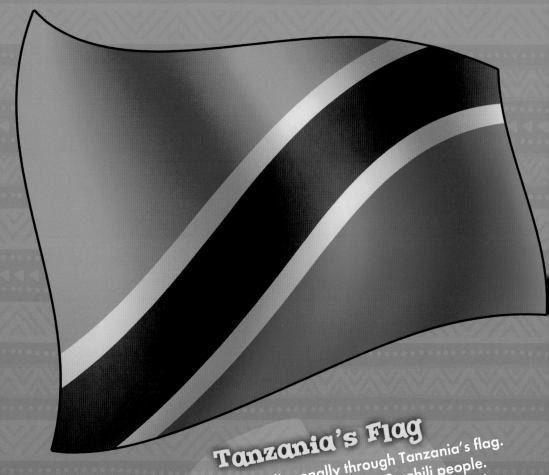

Tanzania's Flag

A black band runs diagonally through Tanzania's flag. This is a symbol for the country's Swahili people. Yellow stripes on either side stand for its natural resources. The green upper left corner is a symbol for Tanzania's plants and crops. The blue bottom corner stands for its bodies of water and the Indian Ocean. Tanzania adopted this flag in 1964.

Official Name: United Republic of Tanzania

Area: 365,755 square miles (947,300 square kilometers); Tanzania is the 31st largest country in the world.

Capital City:	Dodoma
Important Cities:	Dar es Salaam, Mwanza
Population:	51,045,882 (July 2015)
Official Languages:	Swahili and English
National Holiday:	Union Day (April 26)
Religions:	Muslim (35%), native beliefs (35%), Christian (30%)
Major Industries:	farming, tourism, mining
Natural Resources:	gemstones, gold, iron, tin, coal, natural gas
Manufactured Products:	wood products, cement, fabric, food products
Farm Products:	bananas, cashews, coffee beans, corn, milk, rice, sorghum, tea, beef
Unit of Money:	Tanzanian shilling; the shilling is divided into 100 senti.

Glossary

ancestors—relatives who lived long ago

archaeologists—scientists who study the remains of past civilizations

cassava—a tropical plant with starchy, edible roots

dormant—not showing signs of eruption, but could erupt again

evolved—developed or grew from one thing into another

export—to sell to a different country

fasting—choosing not to eat

migration—the act of traveling from one place to another, often with the seasons

native—originally from a specific place

plains—large areas of flat land

plantains—a type of banana that is less sweet and is usually cooked

plateau—an area of flat, raised land

prehistoric—related to time periods from before written history

rift valley—a long area of low land that was formed by the shifting plates of Earth's crust

rural—related to the countryside

service jobs—jobs that perform tasks for people or businesses

tourists—people who travel to visit another place

traditions—customs, ideas, or beliefs handed down from one generation to the next

volcanoes—holes in the earth; when a volcano erupts, hot, melted rock called lava shoots out.

To Learn More

AT THE LIBRARY

Anniss, Matt. *Jane Goodall and Mary Leakey*. New York, N.Y.: Gareth Stevens, 2015.

McKenzie, Precious. *Savannahs*. Vero Beach, Fla.: Rourke Pub. LLC, 2011.

Watson, Galadriel. *Mount Kilimanjaro*. New York, N.Y.: AV2 by Weigl, 2014.

ON THE WEB

Learning more about Tanzania is as easy as 1, 2, 3.

1. Go to www.factsurfer.com.

2. Enter "Tanzania" into the search box.

3. Click the "Surf" button and you will see a list of related web sites.

With factsurfer.com, finding more information is just a click away.

Index

The images in this book are reproduced through the courtesy of: Charles Bowman/ Age Fotostock, front cover; Peter Hermes Furian, pp. 4-5; mdd, p. 6; Ulrich Doering/ Alamy, p. 7; Gil.K, pp. 8-9; Independent Picture Service/ Getty Images, pp. 10-11; Nick Garbutt/ SuperStock, p. 10 (top); Wolfgang Kaehler/ SuperStock, p. 10 (middle); James Hager/ robertharding/ SuperStock, p. 10 (bottom); Magdalena Paluchowska, p. 12; Benny Marty, p. 14; Peter Groenendijk / robertharding/ SuperStock, p. 15; Dietmar Temps, pp. 16-17; ton koene/ Alamy, p. 18; Jake Lyell/ Alamy, pp. 19 (left), 23 (left); Joerg Boethling/ Alamy, p. 19 (right); Mark Davidson/ Alamy, p. 20; Nigel Pavitt/ Alamy, p. 21; Charles O. Cecil/ Alamy, p. 22; GunnerL, p. 23 (right); Xinhua/ Alamy, pp. 24-25; Liba Taylor/ Alamy, pp. 26-27; Ogen, p. 29.